C000259161

To Heather,

A little book of

"Angels"

from me to you ! x

Love
Rachel xx x

23.10.2006 .

Edited by *Margaret Lannamann*

Illustrated by *Lisa Parett*

Ariel Books

**Andrews McMeel
Publishing**

Kansas City

angels

Angels copyright © 2003 by Armand Eisen. All rights reserved. Printed in China. No part of this book may be used or reproduced in any manner whatsoever without written permission except in the case of reprints in the context of reviews. For information write Andrews McMeel Publishing, an Andrews McMeel Universal company, 4520 Main Street, Kansas City, Missouri 64111.

Illustrations © 2003 by Lisa Parett

ISBN: 0-7407-3871-2

Library of Congress Catalog Card Number: 2003102677

Angels

We see them on television and in the movies, we *hear* about them in music, art, and literature. But usually, we're too busy to stop and let their *presence* into our lives.

We're too distracted by the hustle and bustle of work and family to let their voices into our *hearts.*

But if we just slow down a bit, we can learn to see beyond the details of our day-to-day living. And at that very moment, we'll discover that our

angels

angels are with us, ready to surround us with their *healing powers* of comfort, protection, and love.

angels

may not always come

when you call them,

but they come when

you need them.

—Karen Goldman

Did You

The word
angel means

Know . . .

"messenger"

in Greek.

Finding Your Angel

Lighting a candle and studying the golden flame may open your heart to the message of the angels.

In a moment of grace,

grace,

angels

we can grasp
eternity
in the palm of our hand.

—Marcel Marceau

Absence of proof

is not

p r o o f

of absence.

—Michael Crichton

a n g e l s

You don't have to
study to become an

angel—

just wing it!

—Nicole Beale

There

was a *pause*—just long enough

angels

for an

angel to pass, flying slowly.

—Ronald Firbank

Angels
in
Movies
and
Plays

angels

City of Angels

Angels in America

It's a Wonderful Life

Hell's Angels

Angel in My Pocket

Outside the open window

the morning air is all awash with

angels.

—Richard Wilbur

We all have angels guiding us. . . . They look after us. They heal us, touch us, comfort us with invisible warm hands. . . . What will bring their help? Asking. Giving thanks.

—Sophy Burnham

angels

Those who
walk with
angels
learn to soa

angels

above the clouds.

—Margaret Neylon

'Tis only when they spring

to heaven that

angel's

Reveal themselves to you.

—Robert Browning

angels

The guardian angels of life

sometimes fly so high as to be

beyond our sight, but they are

always looking down

upon us.

—Jean Paul Richter

Did You

Sometimes

we receive messages

from angels in our

sleep, especially

know . . .

around four in the
morning—the most
psychic time
of day.

ANGELS

are always jus

angels

utside the front door.

—Karen Goldman

Finding Your Angel

You may realize

you have been

visited by an

angel only after

she has gone.

Joy is prayer—

Joy is strength—

Joy is love—

Joy is a net of love

by which you can

catch souls.

—Mother Teresa

Did You

The four
archangels
are named

now . . .

Michael,

Gabriel,

Raphael,

and Uriel.

I dwell in Possib

angels

ity. . .

—Emily Dickinson

The angel was trained f

ve, she was disciplined in *love* . . .

—Marianne Williamson

Finding Your Angel

When you are faced
with a difficult
choice, try to keep
yourself on the side
of the angels.

Did You

October 2

is a day set aside by

many to recognize the

...now . . .

care to us given

by our guardian

angels.

Angels in Television

angels

Touched By an Angel

Angel

Charlie's Angels

Finding Your Angel

Remember that you're never alone—your guardian angel is always there with you.

I got a whole angel chorus up there humming. I really believe angels are happiest when you're happy.

—Denise Rich

It is a sign that in this place, as in *heaven,* all things grow with grace and are in rhyme.

—Duane Michaels

Did You

Angels appear in the
work of such famous
writers as John Milton,
Dante Alighieri,
William Shakespeare,
William Blake,

Know . . .

Mark Twain,

Robert Browning,

John Keats,

Leo Tolstoy, and

Isaac Bashevis Singer.

We couldn't conceive of a *miracle* if none
had ever happened.

—Libbie Fudim

angels

The very presence of an angel
is a communication. Even when an
angel crosses our path in silence,
God has said to us, "I am here.
I am present in your
life."

—Tobias Palmer

Finding
Your
Angel

The wings of an angel

at work on earth may

be hidden from our

eyes.

Trust the wings you have been given

angels

u have earned them. You do know how to fly.

—Karen Goldman

Did You

Some
people who
have experienced
the presence of an

Know . . .

angel describe
the experience as
musical or aromatic,
rather than visual.

Finding Your Angel

Hang a wreath of dried yarrow wrapped with copper wire in your home to strengthen communication with your inner angel.

Finding Your Angel

If you wish you felt the presence of your angel more often, make sure you're keeping your mind receptive and your heart open.

Everyone

can be an

a n g

angels

e l.

—Cindy Crawford

Angels
in
Geography

angels

Angel Falls, Venezuela

Angel Island, California

Mount Angel, Oregon

Los Angeles, California

Angel Fire, New Mexico

and then I

heard the wonderful singing

angels

of many angels.

—Bridget of Sweden

Did You

Ancient records suggest that descriptions of angels existed as far back as six thousand years ago, when winged human

Know . . .

forms called *kabiru*
kept watch over the
civilizations of
Mesopotamia and
Sumeria.

I believe that when
you lose a person you
love, you gain an

angel

you know.

—Oprah Winfrey

Book design and composition

by Diane Hobbing of

SNAP-HAUS GRAPHICS

in Dumont, NJ